69

69 TRICKS TO TRAVELLING

JON DUTTON + KATHY READY

A.

ABSOLUTE PRESS

First published in Great Britain in 2004 by
Absolute Press
Scarborough House, 29 James Street West
Bath BA1 2BT, England
Phone 44 (0) 1225 316013 **Fax** 44 (0) 1225 445836
E-mail info@absolutepress.co.uk
Web www.absolutepress.co.uk

A catalogue record of this book is available from the British Library

ISBN 1 9045473 11 8

Printed and bound in Italy by Legoprint

Also available:
69 ESSENTIAL WORDS FOR TRAVELLERS
69 USES FOR A WATER BOTTLE

For all the people we have met on our travels

The unknowns are why we travel. To see and feel what lies in foreign lands.

But the unknown also brings feelings of trepidation.

69 Tricks to Travelling aims to ease away the fear and agitation common to jetting off to and setting foot in foreign countries.

Advice on which essential items to take, how to make life on the road more comfortable, priceless safety tips, and how to handle yourself in foreign cultures.

For the seasoned traveller, it serves as a checklist for packing; for the backpacking novice, it offers and insight into new ideas and ways to travel.

happy travels

01	P.M.T.	23	MEDICAL KIT
02	TORCH	24	MOSQUITO REPELLENT
03	ROSEMARY OIL	25	GINGER
04	COMPACT BACK PACK	26	HAND TOWELS
05	VACUUM-PACKED FLEECE	27	VISAS
		28	CANDLES
06	HAIR BANDS	29	GARLIC
07	FLIP FLOPS	30	MAP
08	WATCH OUT FOR SCAMS	31	SOCKS
		32	WATER BOTTLE HOLDER
09	SUNSCREEN	33	PEEL FRUIT AND EAT COOKED VEGETABLES
10	POCKET KNIFE		
11	LIP BALM	34	BLOOD TYPE
12	LAVENDER OIL	35	CHECK FOR BED BUGS
13	EAR PLUGS	36	BOOK
14	LIGHTER	37	EXTRA CASH STASH
15	WASHING POWDER	38	TOILET PAPER
16	E-MAIL ADDRESS	39	SPIRULINA
17	TIE YOUR SHOELACES	40	MOSQUITO NET
18	CONDOMS	41	PADLOCKS AND BAG CHAIN
19	PERMETHRIN		
20	MONEY BELT	42	ALARM CLOCK
21	PEGS	43	THERMOMETER
22	DRINK GOOD WATER		

CONTENTS

P. M. T.

Passport, Money, Tickets. Seems like a logical addition to your travelling pack, but you'd be surprised how many people forget one or all of these things!

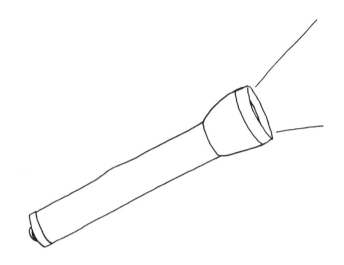

torch

an essential travel item to
shed light on a dark
situation. Always keep it
close at night — even under
your pillow. Mini-Maglites
are ideal as they are
light and compact.

rosemary oil

rosemary has a stimulating effect on the nervous system. It gives mental clarity and boosts the confidence - good when you're tired but have to keep going! It improves the circulation, having a warming effect on cold, limbs and is excellent for tired, over worked muscles.

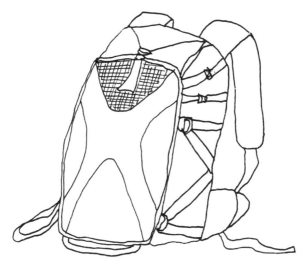

compact
back pack

this is essential for easy travel.
You don't want to be carrying a
pack that is too heavy and too
difficult to store on public transport.
There is no need to take lots of
clothes and extras with you !! Look
at the climate you are going to and
take into account that in most
cases it will be cheaper to
buy there.

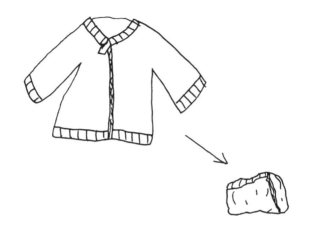

Vacuum-packed fleece

instead of having your favourite
fleece take up all the space in
your pack when travelling from
warm to cold countries, have
it vacuum-packed for easy
storage and open it up
when you need it.

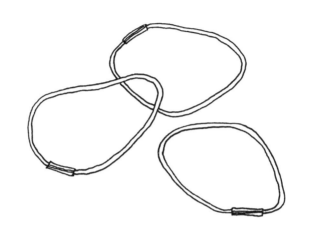

hair bands

Can be used to tame fly away hair, but also in the same way as a rubber band — use it for sealing bags, binding things together, fastening a torch to the bed head...

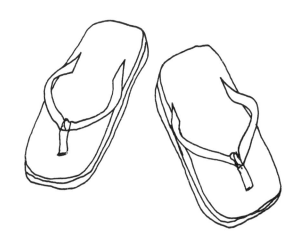

flip flops

take a pair of cheap
flip flops to wear in the
showers to prevent tinea
and other fungal
infections.

watch out for scams

as a traveller in a foreign country, there will always be people wanting to take you for a ride, so follow this simple rule - if it sounds too good to be true it generally is!!

25

UVA/UVB

Sun Screen

make sure it is a minimum of 15+, 30+ in hotter climates. Buying locally ensures you get the right cover for the country you're in.

Pocket knife

an essential item for every traveller's kit. Make sure it has a knife, bottle opener, cork screw, screw driver, tweezers and a can opener.

lip balm

Make sure it contains sunscreen. Lip balm is particularly good for the prevention of wind burn when sitting in open cars/trucks etc.

lavender oil

apply neat to cuts, bruises and burns to accelerate healing and reduce pain, redness and swelling. Rub a little oil on your temples and back of your neck for headaches. Also use lavender as a relaxant. It will settle the nerves and give you a sound night's sleep.

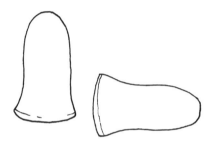

ear plugs

a lot of cities are
extremely noisy and
sometimes using ear plugs
is the only way to get
some sleep.

lighter

a self explanatory
useful addition to your
travelling kit — smoker
or not!

washing powder

it is often expensive to get your clothes washed and most times it's easier to wash them yourself. Take washing powder with you or buy it in any market place. Store it in empty film canisters to keep dry and better utilize storage space.

email address

having an email address is essential
for contact with family, friends, and
other travellers. It's a good idea
to scan a copy of your passport,
birth certificate, insurance etc and
save it to your email address
in case of an emergency.

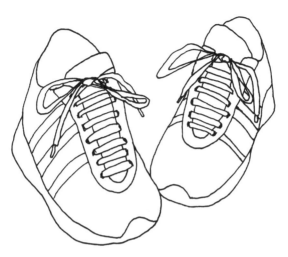

tie
your shoelaces

always make sure your shoe laces
are tied. One of the most common
ways of catching dysentery is people
going to the toilet in the middle of the
night and not bothering to tie their
shoe laces — the next morning they
tie them before breakfast.

condoms

apart from the obvious...
Condoms can be used as a storage
container for sugar, coffee, washing
powder and anything else you
fancy — tie a knot in the
end or seal with an
elastic band.

permethrin

can be bought from most travel/
outdoor stores. Spray on your
clothing and mosquito net for
protection against mosquitoes
ticks, mites and over 100 other
insects. It lasts up to 5 washes.

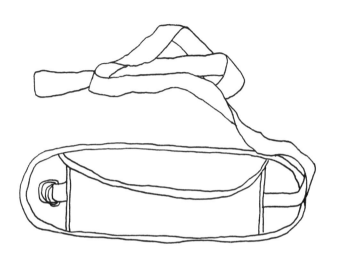

money belt

a money belt that sits flat across
your stomach can be bought from
most travel/outdoor stores and is
usually tan or black in colour.
keep your passport, traveller's
cheques and larger sums of cash
safe, by wearing it at all times
hidden underneath your clothing.

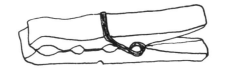

Pegs

2 or 3 should be enough.
Use them for hanging
any number of things.

drink
good water

when buying bottled water, make sure
the seal is not broken. If boiling water
for purification, boil for 1 minute at low
altitudes, 3 minutes over 2000m. Iodine
tablets should only be used sparingly
as too much iodine is toxic to the
body and it doesn't kill all
contaminants.

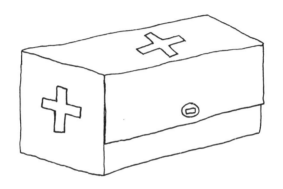

medical kit

make sure it is small and compact. most pharmacies and outdoor stores stock a varied range to suit your needs.

Sun glasses

apart from u.v. protection, sunglasses are also essential for dusty roads and beaches and security whilst sleeping on buses,, trains etc as people can't see if you're asleep or not. Take them off when talking to locals, as eye contact is essential.

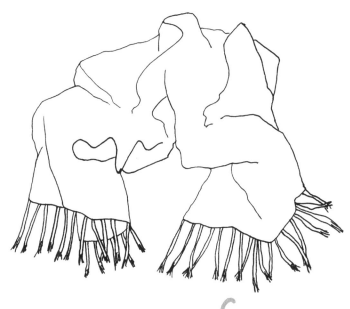

scarf

a light scarf is a useful item in both
hot and cold climates — make sure it is at
least 4 feet long so it can be wrapped
around a few times for warmth and
protection. Use it to cover your face
on dusty roads and moisten with
water to keep you cool. Most
countries sell a good variety at a
cheap price.

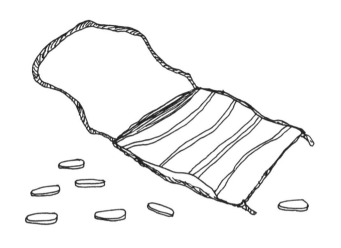

Cash wallet

keep a separate wallet to your passport, travellers cheques etc for a small amount of local currency. Conceal it under your shirt and around your neck to deter thieves but also allow easy access This suggests to locals that you do not have alot of money and if you do get mugged, the cash wallet can be handed over without the loss of all your valuables.

shaving oil

an ideal companion for easy shaving whilst travelling. No need to use hot water as the oil softens the skin, preventing nicks and razor burn. It comes in a tiny bottle that wont take up space in your pack.

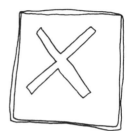

learn local graces

make a point of respecting the culture you're in by learning the local graces - don't wear revealing clothing, remove shoes when entering temples, don't touch children's heads, don't point your feet at people when seated... this will give you greater insight into the culture you're visiting as well as respect from the local people.

tiger balm

excellent for bites and stings.
Inhale for relief from
travel sickness and rub
into the skin to soothe
sore muscles.

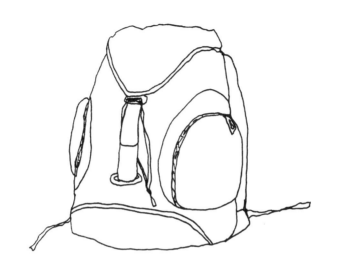

day Pack

a necessity for easy
day journeys, shopping
sightseeing etc.

Small gifts

Carry some small gifts to give to people you meet. Postcards of the country you are from are good and pens and paper are always appreciated in developing countries —a far healthier exchange than giving out money.

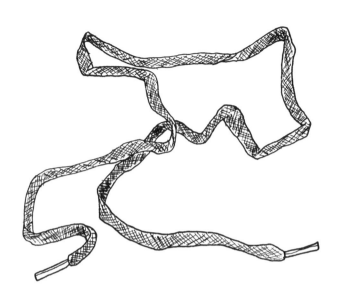

Shoelaces

Carry a spare set of laces with you as they are good for lashing extra belongings onto your back pack, extending mosquito net fastenings, hanging items in your room etc. And, have the added bonus of being used as shoe laces should your original ones snap!

sewing kit

a handy addition to your pack for sewing up torn clothes, rips in your bag and holes in your mosquito net.

travel insurance

read the fine print and make sure you know what you're covered for — white water rafting, scuba diving, bungy jumping, wintersports etc. leave a photocopy of your policy at home and keep a list of your traveller's cheque numbers with it.

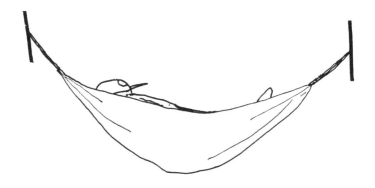

hammock

a hammock is a versatile addition to your pack. It can be strung up when there is a shortage of chairs, be used as a bed and is good to ward of sea sickness. Look for a nylon commando style as it's light weight and easily stored. Buy locally for a better price.

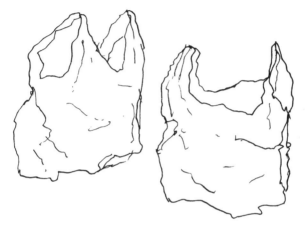

Plastic bags

handy for storage but also for waterproofing. Use them to protect your clothing and keep travellers cheques, money and passport safe from moisture in your money belt.

embassy
phone numbers

make sure you have the phone
number of your embassy in the
country/ countries you're
travelling to. Write it down
somewhere safe.

rehydration salts

essential when travelling in countries
with poor hygiene. use to rehydrate
yourself when suffering from diarrhoea
and vomiting. When hiking the salts
can also be used if your water
supply is limited — adding a little to
your water will stop you needing
to drink as much.

sarong

a cotton sarong — apart from taking you to the heights of fashion on the beach — saves you having to pack a towel. It is a light-weight, compactable and quick-drying alternative. Buy locally for a cheaper and larger variety.

write insurance numbers in shoe

It's a good idea to write down your insurance details, passport number and credit card emergency phone number on a piece of paper (protected in plastic) and put it under the inner sole of your shoe for quick and easy access.

tea-tree oil

tea-tree or ti-tree oil is a
strong antibiotic, antiviral and
antiseptic. Use it for burns, sores,
sunburn, ringworm, warts, tinea,
herpes and athletes foot. It can
also be inhaled to help fight coughs,
colds and infection and be used
to treat thrush.

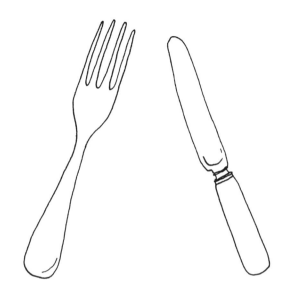

clean cutlery

It's a good idea to give your cutlery a quick wipe before use with a dampened serviette. This will enhance your chances of a healthy journey — don't feel embarrassed as it's common for the locals to do this too!

mosquito coils

light near the door and
windows of your room
at sunset. Buy locally
to stop them getting
crushed in your pack!

hola

Konnichiha

namaste

sawatdee kaa

bonjour

ciao

learn
local language

at least learn how to say
'hello', 'goodbye' and 'thank you'.
If you make some effort the locals
are generally more open and
accepting of you and you'll
get a better understanding
of the culture you're in.

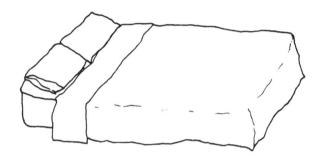

sheets
and pillow cases

take a double if travelling as a couple
as most guest houses have a double bed
or 2 singles that can be pushed
together. If travelling on your own, sew a
double sheet down one side to create
a 'sleeping sack! This will act as 2
sheets but only take the space
of one in your pack.

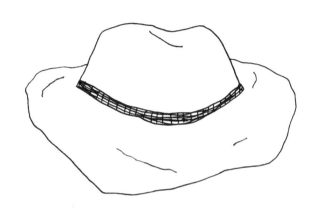

hat

we all know how sunburn
and sunstroke can ruin your
travels, so pack a cotton hat in
a light colour to protect you.
Make sure it has a brim to stop
your neck from burning.

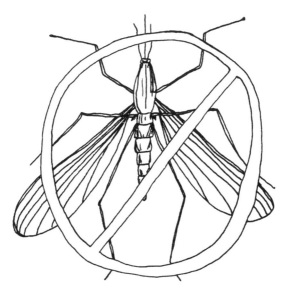

mosquito repellent

Make sure the repellent contains DEET. Less than 35% DEET is recommended as this is just as effective as higher concentrations but with less risk of toxicity. Spray ankles, wrists, hands and neck for protection — sunrise and sunset are the key times mosquitoes come out to feed.

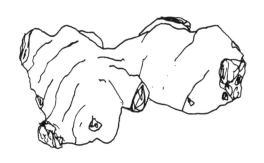

ginger

Combats nausea, car sickness,
sea sickness etc. Use it for the
treatment of wind and as a
tonic for the digestive system.
Make fresh ginger tea by
slicing root ginger into a cup
of boiled water.

hand towels

avoid using them! It is much safer to carry some toilet paper to dry your hands on than using an existing hand towel in areas of poor hygiene.

visas

find out if a visa is needed and if so which type, BEFORE you embark on your travels. Also check how long the visa is valid before you must enter the country you're going to. Obtaining visas in foreign countries can save money, but you'll have to spend a few days waiting, which you may not want to do at the time.

candles

a handy item to call on
when the power goes out, but
also useful for creating a
softer atmosphere
outside or in.

garlic

garlic contains 4 different types of natural antibiotic. Use it to fight colds, flu and chest infections. Add it to your food whenever possible and when sick, ingest a whole clove of garlic in a tablespoon of sweet honey — the honey allows you to swallow the garlic uncrushed, therefore preventing it from passing out of your body and giving garlic breath.

map

It's a good idea to have a map of the region you're in eg. Laos, Thailand and Vietnam incorporated into one map. This allows you to plot routes between countries, get off the beaten track, and estimate travelling times.

Socks

cotton socks are best as they
allow your feet to breathe, are
not bulky and dry quickly. They
can be worn with flip flops in hot
climates when the temperature drops
in the evening a little, and can be
layered in cold climates for
extra warmth.

water bottle holder

allows easy access to water
without having to rummage
around in your bag. Most
countries sell a variety
of designs.

Peel fruit and eat cooked vegetables

Play it safe by only eating cooked vegetables and fruit that has to be peeled or can be peeled easily with a knife.

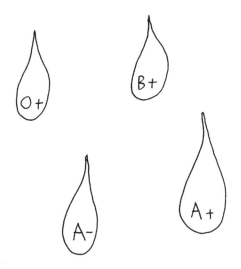

blood type

write down your blood
type and keep it somewhere
safe — you never know
when or where you
might need it.

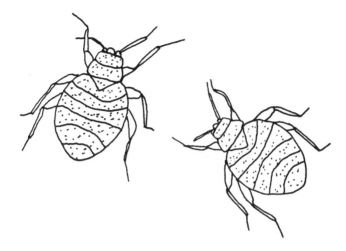

check for
bed bugs

blood stains on your mattress is a
sign that bed bugs are present.
So too is dark spotting in the crevice
of the bed frame. Fleas can also
cause problems - place a white piece of
paper on the floor, if you can see
fleas jumping onto the paper !!
book another room !!

book

a great way to keep you entertained on long journeys. Try to find a book about, or set in the country you're in — this will make sight seeing more interesting and give you a feel for the culture. Swap books with fellow travellers to lighten your load and enhance your reading repertoire.

extra cash stash

keep $50 U.S. stashed away for
an emergency, as it can be changed
in any country. Seal it watertight
in plastic and keep it in the sole
of your shoe, underneath the
inner sole. This will enable you to
get transport to an embassy, food,
accomodation etc, should
everything go missing.

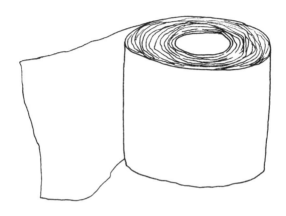

toilet paper

always carry some — it can
be used as a serviette or
tissue and you never
know when you might
be left short!!

Spirulina

Spirulina is a complete source of practically all the nutrients the body needs. It's an excellent booster for vegetarians and particularly good when travelling in regions where it is hard to get a hearty meal.

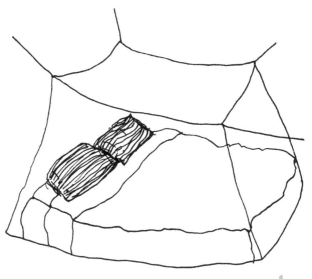

mosquito net

Buy a double if travelling as a couple, otherwise a single is sufficient. Make sure it has 4 points for hanging, not a single at the top, as it is easier to find things to tie the net to.

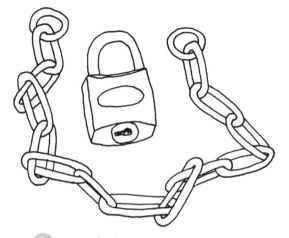

Padlocks and bag chain

Use padlocks to secure your bags shut as well as the door to your room — many guesthouses have latches so you can lock your room with your own padlock and keys. Use a chain to lock your bag to seats or the roof of buses. This is particularly useful in India and South America.

alarm clock

a small, light weight alarm clock is best. Make sure it has a light or glow-in-the-dark hands so you can always see what time it is — better than missing that bus or early morning flight!

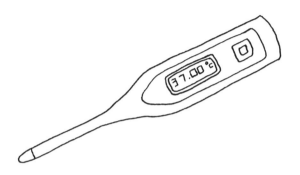

thermometer

an essential life saver. A good quality
non-mecury thermometer is invaluable.
The normal body temperature is
37°c or 98·6°F — a decline or rise in
this temperature by more than 1-2
degrees signifies ill health and
can be fatal.

tobacco and cigarettes

Can be used to bribe, start conversations and be given away as a good will gesture.
It is a great ice breaker when trying to obtain information.

Peppermint oil

excellent for stomach upsets (put 1-2 drops in boiling water or black tea) Inhale it for the treatment of nausea, headaches and respiratory ailments. Dilute with water to soothe itching, inflammation and sunburn.